COMMON CENTS

THE TOTALLY APPROACHABLE, NOT-SCARY GUIDES

COMMON CENTS

A BUDGET WORKBOOK

MELEAH BOWLES AND **ELISE WILLIAMS**

THE CREATORS OF *EARN SPEND LIVE*

ROCK
POINT

Inspiring | Educating | Creating | Entertaining

Brimming with creative inspiration, how-to projects, and useful information to enrich your everyday life, Quarto Knows is a favorite destination for those pursuing their interests and passions. Visit our site and dig deeper with our books into your area of interest: Quarto Creates, Quarto Cooks, Quarto Homes, Quarto Lives, Quarto Drives, Quarto Explores, Quarto Gifts, or Quarto Kids.

First published in 2019 by Rock Point,
an imprint of The Quarto Group
142 West 36th Street, 4th Floor
New York, NY 10018 USA
T (212) 779-4972 **F** (212) 779-6058
www.QuartoKnows.com

Designed by Katie Cooper
Illustrations by Jasmine Av

Race Point Publishing titles are also available at discount for retail, wholesale, promotional, and bulk purchase. For details, contact the Special Sales Manager by email at specialsales@quarto.com or by mail at The Quarto Group, Attn: Special Sales Manager, 100 Cummings Center Suite 265D, Beverly, MA 01915, USA.

10 9 8 7 6

ISBN: 978-1-63106-577-4

Editorial Director: Rage Kindelsperger
Managing Editor: Erin Canning
Editor: Keyla Hernández
Cover and Interior Design: Katie Cooper
Illustration Design: Jasmine Av
Design Manager: Phil Buchanan

Printed in China

DEDICATION

To everyone who was as excited about this book as we were.

Especially those who read our first drafts.

—Elise and Meleah

CONTENTS

FORMAL(ISH) INTROS

HAVE YOU sat down and made your first budget? Started paying off your student loans? Applied for your first credit card? Checked your credit score? Opened a savings account? If you haven't done all (or any) of the things on this list yet, rest assured— **you are not alone!**

Have you racked up so much credit card debt you finally learned what "interest" was? Made a huge impulse buy and had to survive on ramen for the next two weeks? Forgotten to pay a few bills? If so, you are *also* not alone. We've probably (definitely) made the same mistakes. Whichever list you have more in common with, you're in the right place.

In this workbook, we'll introduce you to budgets, debt repayment, emergency funds, and financial goals and walk you through everything step by step.

You won't find any financial mumbo jumbo here; we believe in K.I.S.S. (Keep It Simple, Smartie). Because the smartest thing you can do is Keep It Simple.

We'll also be sharing financial advice based on our own personal experiences, discussing the different ways the two of us do things (because, as you'll soon learn, there is no absolute "right" way that works for everyone when it comes to managing finances), and owning up to our own personal financial blunders.

Because if there's one thing we've learned while figuring out how to get our money (and lives in general) together, it's that you always learn the most about how to succeed from making mistakes.

WHAT IS EARN SPEND LIVE?

In 2015, we created Earn Spend Live—a lifestyle website devoted to helping young women navigate their career, manage their finances, and figure out how to be a functioning adult. At the time, we were navigating our first jobs post-college and figuring everything out as we went—how much of our paychecks to save, how much to spend, how much to contribute to a 401k, etc.

As we stumbled along, we wished we had some kind of guide to help us understand the financial decisions we were making—aside from the typical advice you find online for millennials, like skipping our morning lattes and avocado toast and giving up any dreams of owning our own homes.

So with a push from our mentor, who believes in us far too much, we decided to make our own guide—aka Earn Spend Live—where we detail our own successes and mistakes, as well as provide advice from women much more successful than us.

We are by no means financial experts, and we've never pretended to be; we're just two twentysomethings faking it til' we make it, like you.

However, we've learned a lot from the research we've done creating Earn Spend Live, the interviews we've conducted, guest posts written by financial experts, and all of the mistakes we've made along the way.

(Plus, you'll find a few words of wisdom from experts sprinkled throughout this book; so you don't just have to take our word.)

Fast forward to a few years later and we're financially smarter than we used to be. (Or at least this book deal has given us more confidence so we sound smarter.) Because you picked up this book and made it this far, we're assuming you want to be financially smarter, too.

And if your parents bought this for you, we're assuming their gift is a not-so-subtle hint that they want you to stop sucking the life out of their bank account and get financially smart.

Some other assumptions we're making:

• You're a legal adult, with responsibilities and bills to pay.

• You have a bank account.

• You have a desire (no matter how small) to improve your finances.

Assuming our assumptions are correct, we're ready to get this show on the road.

Side note: We may have written this book, but now that you've bought it, it's yours and you can use it however you want. If you already have a digital budgeting system that you love, then keep using it. If you're a goal-setting fanatic, flip to chapter five and start setting some goals.

If you're not sure what you're doing or what life even means anymore, just stick with us page by page and we'll help you out.

ELISE

"As coauthors, we're in this together—but we each have a few individual nuggets of advice. Look for our faces for some individual tips, tricks, mistakes, and lessons learned!"

MELEAH

FINANCIAL SELF-ASSESSMENT

Now that you know us, let's get to know you!

Before you can figure out exactly where you want to improve financially, you need to take a hard look at the current state of your finances.

In the following worksheet, we've provided a space for you to record whether or not you currently have a budget, how much is in your savings and emergency fund, your current credit score, and the amount of debt you currently have.

Once you have these numbers written down in front of you, setting financial goals should be a breeze—but we'll get to that later.

We've also provided a similar worksheet at the end of the book so you can see how much your finances have improved when you're done!

1. Do you have a budget?

| YES | NO |

2. Do you have a savings account?

| YES | NO |

If yes, how much money is in your savings account?

_____

3. Do you have an emergency fund?

| YES | NO |

If yes, how much money is in your emergency fund?

_____

4. What's your current credit score?

_____

5. Do you have debt?

| YES | NO |

If yes, how much do you owe?

_____

CHAPTER ONE

BUDGETING BREAKDOWN

A BUDGET IS *HELLA* IMPORTANT. Between paying your rent, keeping your pet alive, saving for your future, and not starving to death, your money goes a lot of different places—and fast. The days of dreading the state of your bank account after a night out should be over; hate to break it to you, but you're an adult now, so it's time to start tracking your spending like one.

The first step of making a budget is to take an inventory of your finances—namely, your income (aka money in) and expenses (aka money out).

How old were we when we made our first budget?

"When I was probably 11 years old, I really wanted a cell phone. My parents basically said, 'We're not buying you a cell phone, but you can buy one.' So I did a whole budget starting with all of my expenses (vending machine Cokes and Pop Tarts) and all of my income ($1 week allowance and irregular chore money). Long story short, I could not, in fact, afford a cell phone, but I did learn that you need to have more income than you have expenses."

"My dad has always been a real penny-pincher, so I grew up being familiar with budgets. But it wasn't until I moved out of my parents' house (for the second time) at 23 and started paying *all* of my own bills that I actually pulled up Google Sheets and color coded my way to my first real budget (and showed it to my dad and Meleah for a second and third set of eyes). Meleah's story makes me look dumb, but this just goes to show it's never too early, or late, to get your finances in order."

To get started, we suggest pulling up (and maybe printing out) your bank statement (and your credit card statement, for good measure) for the past month, and keeping it handy for the next few steps.

HOW TO USE *ALL BILLS*

Using your bank and credit card statements, make a list of your bills, including annual and monthly. All of them. Don't hide them, don't crumple them up in your purse, don't avoid opening the emails; write them down in the All Bills worksheet. And then cry a little inside. Or outside, no one has to know.

Filling out your All Bills worksheet can be quasi-traumatic because expenses like rent, a mortgage, and health insurance are pretty fixed—and expensive. If some of your bills vary month to month, like utilities and electric, just take an average from the past three months and write it down; then make a note that it's subject to change. Think of this list of bills as the core of your budget (you'll end up copying them over to your monthly budget as well); it won't change as much as your monthly budget, where you can trim things if you need to cut down on spending.

We've also included checkboxes for you to track whether your payment will come out of your checking account or be paid by credit card, as well as some blank lines for you to fill in if you need them—for extra credit cards, student loans, annual gym membership fees, annual pet check-ups, etc. So get all of your actual bills down on paper, add up your total bills amount, and then let's move on to the next step.

"The only reason I use a credit card for some of my payments is because a credit card is safer to use for online payments. Proceed with caution!"

Before creating your monthly budget, have these things in front of you:

☐ **Bank statements**
☐ **Credit card statements**
☐ **All Bills (filled out)**

BILLS	AMOUNT	DUE	CHECKING	CRE

MONTHLY

BILLS	AMOUNT	DUE	CHECKING	CRE
RENT/MORTGAGE	$_____	_____	☐	☐
PROPERTY INSURANCE	$_____	_____	☐	☐
UTILITIES	$_____	_____	☐	☐
INTERNET	$_____	_____	☐	☐
PHONE BILL	$_____	_____	☐	☐
HEALTH INSURANCE	$_____	_____	☐	☐
TRANSPORTATION	$_____	_____	☐	☐
_____	$_____	_____	☐	☐
_____	$_____	_____	☐	☐
_____	$_____	_____	☐	☐

DEBT

BILLS	AMOUNT	DUE	CHECKING	CRE
CREDIT CARD 1	$_____	_____	☐	☐
CREDIT CARD 2	$_____	_____	☐	☐
STUDENT LOANS	$_____	_____	☐	☐
_____	$_____	_____	☐	☐
_____	$_____	_____	☐	☐
_____	$_____	_____	☐	☐

MISC.

BILLS	AMOUNT	DUE	CHECKING	CRE
MEMBERSHIPS	$_____	_____	☐	☐
TAXES	$_____	_____	☐	☐
_____	$_____	_____	☐	☐
_____	$_____	_____	☐	☐
_____	$_____	_____	☐	☐
_____	$_____	_____	☐	☐

TOTAL BILLS $_____

ALL BILLS

HOW TO USE *MONTHLY BUDGET*

Next, flip to the Monthly Budget worksheets (we've included thirteen so you'll have one as a template and one for each month for a year) and write down all of your other monthly expenses. This is where you will track exactly where all of your money goes each month—from more responsible spending, like paying off your credit card(s) and saving for retirement, to more fun expenses, like how much money you spent on dining out or on new makeup at Sephora.

It's also worth noting that your budget will be different from your friend's, or even your roommate's. There are some universal truths when it comes to budgeting, but ultimately it's *your* life, *your* money, and *you* need to figure out how to best manage it. The two of us, for example, have slightly different budgets—and we wrote this book together (with only a few minor disagreements).

Because everyone makes different money choices, we left you A LOT of blank spaces for however you choose to spend your money each month. In fact, when we initially asked our friends to workshop the first draft of these budgeting worksheets, someone asked us, "Where would I include a gym membership?" We immediately gave each other looks and started cackling; not because we purposely left that off the list, but because we definitely don't have gym memberships, and so needing a spot for it had literally never crossed our minds during our initial run-through.

So, if you need space to budget for the gym, workout equipment, or supplements, add it in. If you need to budget for a monthly spray tan, add it in. We both have several line items devoted to our pet expenses in our personal budgets, so if you're a pet parent, be sure to budget for vet bills, food, litter, toys, the works.

The point is, while this budget does include plenty of fixed, universal expenses, you can completely customize it to budget for your lifestyle.

Your first pass through your expenses doesn't have to be perfect. As exemplified with the gym membership scenario, we accidentally left a few items off of our first pass at

MAKING this budget worksheet, so you'll be fine. Perfection is the enemy of good, and all that jazz.

Pro Tip: You might want to write in pencil! Or keep your correction tape close by if you just *need* to write in pen.

You should be updating and re-evaluating your budget pretty frequently anyway (if you move, get a promotion, or change jobs, for example), so you can always go back and add to it. A word of caution, or wisdom, or what have you: **Some bills will change month to month.**

"I moved into an apartment all by myself (plus my cat) for the first time at 25. I had always been used to splitting rent, bills, and groceries with someone else. So when all my payments doubled, I had to redo my entire budget ASAP. Then a couple of months later, I got a promotion—so I had to re-evaluate my budget again. You never know where life will take you financially (or when), so you (and your budget) have to be flexible."

"'My bills just change too much right now!' is an actual excuse I've used to avoid making a budget before. This is not a good excuse, and since then I've learned an imperfect budget is better than no budget. Don't be like past-Meleah. Do your budget anyway."

If you don't have a completely and totally accurate average, that's fine for now. Just start out by making an educated guess (like we said earlier, you can average your payments from the last three or so months). If you find that you spend more or less on something each month, adjust as needed.

Plus, we've dedicated a space for notes about each line item; so if you want to note that a certain bill will change month to month, write it down. If you have auto-draft set up for a couple of payments, go ahead and write that down too!

We've also included a monthly overall "Goals" section. Here, you can write down three things you want to accomplish that month. This could be something you want to cut back spending on (do you *really* need that mani-pedi this month?), or it could even be putting back a little extra into your savings and/or emergency fund.

"I have a major online shopping problem, so I like to do no-spending challenges every few months. You can also do no-spending challenges with coffee, travel, or dining out—plus, you can alternate and do a different one each month! (See, budgeting can be fun...kind of.)"

If you're feeling a little lost when you peek at the monthly goal boxes, check out chapter 5, "Setting Financial Goals." (Remember: you're free to jump around this workbook a bit; after all, this is about what's best for you and your finances.) You can look at the steps you need to take to accomplish your goals and use your monthly goals as a means to achieve them.

All that being said, the most important aspect of creating a budget is to set financial goals and stick to them (as best you can, at least). On each Monthly Budget worksheet, we've included a "goal" amount for each line item as well as an "actual" amount. Here, you'll set your money goals (although the items on the first page will be fixed amounts for the most part) and then be able to track whether or not you're meeting your goals. After a couple of months you'll really be able to see where you're spending way too much—and where you can cut back.

For example, if you're making your April budget, you might plan to only spend $45 on movies, but when you review your spending from April, you might see that you've spent $65. If it's a one-time thing, don't sweat it, but if after a couple of months you see that you always overspend at the movie theater, you need to re-evaluate. Maybe the answer is to cut back how often you're going to the theater, or maybe the answer is that you need to look at your budget and find somewhere else you can cut so you can keep on staying current on the latest flicks. Remember: at the end of the day, your budget needs to work for you!

Jason Reposa, CEO of MyBankTracker.com, on Cutting Down Spending:

"Start utilizing self-restraint; if you meet with friends three times a week for dinner, try lowering that number to one time and start having dinner at each other's houses."

If you're a person who likes to have visuals, feel free to highlight and/or color code to your heart's content. If you over-spent on one line item, highlight the amount or circle it in red. (Then make a plan for cutting back next month.) If you were on-goal or you spent less than anticipated, make note of that too and give yourself a little pat on the back! (And even consider reducing that goal amount.)

HOW TO USE *TOTAL MONEY OUT* VS. *TOTAL MONEY IN*

When you're setting your "goal" amount for each line item, be sure you add everything up to make sure you're living within your means (more on that later). If your Total Money Out is more than your Total Money In, you'll need to go back, re-evaluate your priorities for the month, and adjust your budget.

When totalling up your Total Money In, figure out how much money you make each month. Start with your regular, post-tax, take-home pay, and then add in any recurring side-gigs—whether it is freelancing, pet-sitting, or any entrepreneurial endeavors. If you don't know exactly how much you make, refer back to your last several bank statements. If you work an inconsistent schedule or get paid based on commission, the Total Money In figure will be a little harder to come up with, but try to just use an average of the last few months.

Once you've done all the math (which can take a while, so block out a serious chunk of time for this), you can start entering the actual amounts you're spending on each line item. It's important to note that there is NO right way to do this; you can use a pencil and enter in amounts as you go through the month, whether that be weekly or bi-weekly, or even as you make purchases, or you can sit down at the end of the month and track everything at once.

Either way, at the end of the month, total up your spending, aka your Total Money Out. Then subtract that amount from your income, aka your Total Money In.

Take a good, hard look at that final number. Did you spend more than you made? (Thanks, credit cards.) How much more? Or did you spend less than you made? How much less? What are you going to do with that money? What will you do differently next month? (We've included a few notes pages for you at the end of the book—so if you want to answer these questions there, you'll have plenty of space to do so.)

Ideally, you want the amount left at the end of the month to be a positive number. This is called "living within your means." And because you've already factored in things like contributions to savings and retirement, this is a good number.

But if you really want to set yourself up for financial success, you should be living beneath your means as opposed to just within them. Rich people are rich for a reason; they live like they're poor, aka well beneath their means.

This is a concept we learned from Bridget Casey, the founder of Money After Graduation (and our second-favorite Canadian, because, well, Ryan Reynolds exists). She's discussed the concept on her blog, as well as with us on a 2017 episode of our podcast, EVEsdropping.

Bridget Casey, Founder of Money After Graduation, on Living Beneath Your Means:

"At the end of the day, not spending more than you make isn't actually going to get you rich. You're going to have to take more aggressive action with saving, investing, and actually making long-term financial plans if you want to enjoy any financial security. So, it's really awesome if you make a budget and you don't go over every month, but you're really going to need to start doing more than that if you want to enjoy any amount of financial success."

Welcome to the magical, mathematical world of budgeting. It's time-consuming, but it will change your life for the better.

Things to remember when creating your monthly budget:

• Schedule plenty of time.

• Be flexible and keep an eraser handy.

• Set financial goals (and stick to them).

• Keep Total Money In > Total Money Out.

BILLS	GOAL	ACTUAL	CHECKING	CR.

MONTH: _____

MONTHLY

	GOAL	ACTUAL	CHECKING	
RENT / MORTGAGE	$_____	$_____	☐	☐
PROPERTY INSURANCE	$_____	$_____	☐	☐
UTILITIES	$_____	$_____	☐	☐
INTERNET	$_____	$_____	☐	☐
PHONE BILL	$_____	$_____	☐	☐
HEALTH INSURANCE	$_____	$_____	☐	☐
TRANSPORTATION	$_____	$_____	☐	☐
_____	$_____	$_____	☐	☐
_____	$_____	$_____	☐	☐

SAVINGS

	GOAL	ACTUAL	CHECKING	
EMERGENCY FUND	$_____	$_____	☐	☐
RETIREMENT	$_____	$_____	☐	☐
GENERAL SAVINGS	$_____	$_____	☐	☐
_____	$_____	$_____	☐	☐
_____	$_____	$_____	☐	☐

DEBT

	GOAL	ACTUAL	CHECKING	
CREDIT CARD 1	$_____	$_____	☐	☐
CREDIT CARD 2	$_____	$_____	☐	☐
STUDENT LOANS	$_____	$_____	☐	☐
_____	$_____	$_____	☐	☐
_____	$_____	$_____	☐	☐
_____	$_____	$_____	☐	☐
_____	$_____	$_____	☐	☐
_____	$_____	$_____	☐	☐

MONTHLY BUDGET

BILLS	GOAL	ACTUAL	CHECKING	CRED
FOOD				
GROCERIES	$_____	$_____	☐	☐
DINING OUT	$_____	$_____	☐	☐
ALCOHOL	$_____	$_____	☐	☐
COFFEE	$_____	$_____	☐	☐
_____	$_____	$_____	☐	☐
_____	$_____	$_____	☐	☐
EXTRAS				
SELF CARE	$_____	$_____	☐	☐
SHOPPING	$_____	$_____	☐	☐
GIFTS	$_____	$_____	☐	☐
EVENTS	$_____	$_____	☐	☐
TRAVEL	$_____	$_____	☐	☐
CHARITABLE DONATIONS	$_____	$_____	☐	☐
_____	$_____	$_____	☐	☐
_____	$_____	$_____	☐	☐
_____	$_____	$_____	☐	☐
_____	$_____	$_____	☐	☐
_____	$_____	$_____	☐	☐
TOTAL MONEY OUT	$_____			
TAKE-HOME PAY	$_____			
SIDE HUSTLES	$_____			
OTHER	$_____			
TOTAL MONEY IN	$_____			

$$ IN - $$ OUT = $ _____

GOALS

1.

2.

3.

BILLS	GOAL	ACTUAL	CHECKING	CRE

MONTH: _____

MONTHLY

BILLS	GOAL	ACTUAL	CHECKING	
RENT / MORTGAGE	$_____	$_____	☐	☐
PROPERTY INSURANCE	$_____	$_____	☐	☐
UTILITIES	$_____	$_____	☐	☐
INTERNET	$_____	$_____	☐	☐
PHONE BILL	$_____	$_____	☐	☐
HEALTH INSURANCE	$_____	$_____	☐	☐
TRANSPORTATION	$_____	$_____	☐	☐
_____	$_____	$_____	☐	☐
_____	$_____	$_____	☐	☐

SAVINGS

	GOAL	ACTUAL	CHECKING	
EMERGENCY FUND	$_____	$_____	☐	☐
RETIREMENT	$_____	$_____	☐	☐
GENERAL SAVINGS	$_____	$_____	☐	☐
_____	$_____	$_____	☐	☐
_____	$_____	$_____	☐	☐

DEBT

	GOAL	ACTUAL	CHECKING	
CREDIT CARD 1	$_____	$_____	☐	☐
CREDIT CARD 2	$_____	$_____	☐	☐
STUDENT LOANS	$_____	$_____	☐	☐
_____	$_____	$_____	☐	☐
_____	$_____	$_____	☐	☐
_____	$_____	$_____	☐	☐
_____	$_____	$_____	☐	☐
_____	$_____	$_____	☐	☐

NOTES

MONTHLY BUDGET

BILLS	GOAL	ACTUAL	CHECKING	CRE
FOOD				
GROCERIES	$_____	$_____	☐	☐
DINING OUT	$_____	$_____	☐	☐
ALCOHOL	$_____	$_____	☐	☐
COFFEE	$_____	$_____	☐	☐
_____	$_____	$_____	☐	☐
_____	$_____	$_____	☐	☐
EXTRAS				
SELF CARE	$_____	$_____	☐	☐
SHOPPING	$_____	$_____	☐	☐
GIFTS	$_____	$_____	☐	☐
EVENTS	$_____	$_____	☐	☐
TRAVEL	$_____	$_____	☐	☐
CHARITABLE DONATIONS	$_____	$_____	☐	☐
_____	$_____	$_____	☐	☐
_____	$_____	$_____	☐	☐
_____	$_____	$_____	☐	☐
_____	$_____	$_____	☐	☐
_____	$_____	$_____	☐	☐
_____	$_____	$_____	☐	☐

TOTAL MONEY OUT $_____

TAKE-HOME PAY $_____

SIDE HUSTLES $_____

OTHER $_____

TOTAL MONEY IN $_____

$$ IN - $$ OUT = $ _____

_____
_____
_____
_____
_____
_____

_____
_____
_____
_____
_____

_____
_____
_____
_____
_____

GOALS

1.

2.

3.

MONTHLY BUDGET

BILLS	GOAL	ACTUAL	CHECKING	CRE

MONTHLY

MONTH: _____

	GOAL	ACTUAL		
RENT / MORTGAGE	$_____	$_____	☐	☐
PROPERTY INSURANCE	$_____	$_____	☐	☐
UTILITIES	$_____	$_____	☐	☐
INTERNET	$_____	$_____	☐	☐
PHONE BILL	$_____	$_____	☐	☐
HEALTH INSURANCE	$_____	$_____	☐	☐
TRANSPORTATION	$_____	$_____	☐	☐
_____	$_____	$_____	☐	☐
_____	$_____	$_____	☐	☐

SAVINGS

EMERGENCY FUND	$_____	$_____	☐	☐
RETIREMENT	$_____	$_____	☐	☐
GENERAL SAVINGS	$_____	$_____	☐	☐
_____	$_____	$_____	☐	☐
_____	$_____	$_____	☐	☐

DEBT

CREDIT CARD 1	$_____	$_____	☐	☐
CREDIT CARD 2	$_____	$_____	☐	☐
STUDENT LOANS	$_____	$_____	☐	☐
_____	$_____	$_____	☐	☐
_____	$_____	$_____	☐	☐
_____	$_____	$_____	☐	☐
_____	$_____	$_____	☐	☐
_____	$_____	$_____	☐	☐

MONTHLY BUDGET

BILLS	GOAL	ACTUAL	CHECKING	CRE

FOOD

GROCERIES	$_____	$_____	☐	☐
DINING OUT	$_____	$_____	☐	☐
ALCOHOL	$_____	$_____	☐	☐
COFFEE	$_____	$_____	☐	☐
_____	$_____	$_____	☐	☐
_____	$_____	$_____	☐	☐

EXTRAS

SELF CARE	$_____	$_____	☐	☐
SHOPPING	$_____	$_____	☐	☐
GIFTS	$_____	$_____	☐	☐
EVENTS	$_____	$_____	☐	☐
TRAVEL	$_____	$_____	☐	☐
CHARITABLE DONATIONS	$_____	$_____	☐	☐
_____	$_____	$_____	☐	☐
_____	$_____	$_____	☐	☐
_____	$_____	$_____	☐	☐
_____	$_____	$_____	☐	☐
_____	$_____	$_____	☐	☐

TOTAL MONEY OUT	$_____	
TAKE-HOME PAY	$_____	
SIDE HUSTLES	$_____	
OTHER	$_____	
TOTAL MONEY IN	$_____	

$$ IN - $$ OUT = $ _____

_____
_____
_____
_____
_____
_____
_____
_____
_____
_____
_____
_____
_____
_____
_____
_____
_____
_____

GOALS

1.	2.	3.

MONTHLY BUDGET

MONTH: _____

MONTHLY

	GOAL	ACTUAL	CHECKING	
RENT / MORTGAGE	$_____	$_____	☐	☐
PROPERTY INSURANCE	$_____	$_____	☐	☐
UTILITIES	$_____	$_____	☐	☐
INTERNET	$_____	$_____	☐	☐
PHONE BILL	$_____	$_____	☐	☐
HEALTH INSURANCE	$_____	$_____	☐	☐
TRANSPORTATION	$_____	$_____	☐	☐
_____	$_____	$_____	☐	☐
_____	$_____	$_____	☐	☐

SAVINGS

EMERGENCY FUND	$_____	$_____	☐	☐
RETIREMENT	$_____	$_____	☐	☐
GENERAL SAVINGS	$_____	$_____	☐	☐
_____	$_____	$_____	☐	☐
_____	$_____	$_____	☐	☐

DEBT

CREDIT CARD 1	$_____	$_____	☐	☐
CREDIT CARD 2	$_____	$_____	☐	☐
STUDENT LOANS	$_____	$_____	☐	☐
_____	$_____	$_____	☐	☐
_____	$_____	$_____	☐	☐
_____	$_____	$_____	☐	☐
_____	$_____	$_____	☐	☐
_____	$_____	$_____	☐	☐

MONTHLY BUDGET

BILLS	GOAL	ACTUAL	CHECKING	CRE
GROCERIES	$_____	$_____	☐	☐
DINING OUT	$_____	$_____	☐	☐
ALCOHOL	$_____	$_____	☐	☐
COFFEE	$_____	$_____	☐	☐
_____	$_____	$_____	☐	☐
_____	$_____	$_____	☐	☐
SELF CARE	$_____	$_____	☐	☐
SHOPPING	$_____	$_____	☐	☐
GIFTS	$_____	$_____	☐	☐
EVENTS	$_____	$_____	☐	☐
TRAVEL	$_____	$_____	☐	☐
CHARITABLE DONATIONS	$_____	$_____	☐	☐
_____	$_____	$_____	☐	☐
_____	$_____	$_____	☐	☐
_____	$_____	$_____	☐	☐
_____	$_____	$_____	☐	☐
_____	$_____	$_____	☐	☐

FOOD

EXTRAS

TOTAL MONEY OUT $_____

TAKE-HOME PAY $_____

SIDE HUSTLES $_____

OTHER $_____

TOTAL MONEY IN $_____

$$ IN - $$ OUT = $ _____

_____
_____
_____
_____
_____
_____
_____
_____
_____
_____
_____
_____
_____
_____
_____
_____
_____
_____
_____

GOALS

1.

2.

3.

MONTH: _____

MONTHLY

BILLS	GOAL	ACTUAL	CHECKING	CR
RENT / MORTGAGE	$_____	$_____	☐	☐
PROPERTY INSURANCE	$_____	$_____	☐	☐
UTILITIES	$_____	$_____	☐	☐
INTERNET	$_____	$_____	☐	☐
PHONE BILL	$_____	$_____	☐	☐
HEALTH INSURANCE	$_____	$_____	☐	☐
TRANSPORTATION	$_____	$_____	☐	☐
_____	$_____	$_____	☐	☐
_____	$_____	$_____	☐	☐

SAVINGS

	GOAL	ACTUAL	CHECKING	CR
EMERGENCY FUND	$_____	$_____	☐	☐
RETIREMENT	$_____	$_____	☐	☐
GENERAL SAVINGS	$_____	$_____	☐	☐
_____	$_____	$_____	☐	☐
_____	$_____	$_____	☐	☐

DEBT

	GOAL	ACTUAL	CHECKING	CR
CREDIT CARD 1	$_____	$_____	☐	☐
CREDIT CARD 2	$_____	$_____	☐	☐
STUDENT LOANS	$_____	$_____	☐	☐
_____	$_____	$_____	☐	☐
_____	$_____	$_____	☐	☐
_____	$_____	$_____	☐	☐
_____	$_____	$_____	☐	☐
_____	$_____	$_____	☐	☐

MONTHLY BUDGET

BILLS	GOAL	ACTUAL	CHECKING	CR
FOOD				
GROCERIES	$_____	$_____	☐	☐
DINING OUT	$_____	$_____	☐	☐
ALCOHOL	$_____	$_____	☐	☐
COFFEE	$_____	$_____	☐	☐
_____	$_____	$_____	☐	☐
_____	$_____	$_____	☐	☐
EXTRAS				
SELF CARE	$_____	$_____	☐	☐
SHOPPING	$_____	$_____	☐	☐
GIFTS	$_____	$_____	☐	☐
EVENTS	$_____	$_____	☐	☐
TRAVEL	$_____	$_____	☐	☐
CHARITABLE DONATIONS	$_____	$_____	☐	☐
_____	$_____	$_____	☐	☐
_____	$_____	$_____	☐	☐
_____	$_____	$_____	☐	☐
_____	$_____	$_____	☐	☐
_____	$_____	$_____	☐	☐

TOTAL MONEY OUT $_____

TAKE-HOME PAY $_____

SIDE HUSTLES $_____

OTHER $_____

TOTAL MONEY IN $_____

$$ IN - $$ OUT = $ _____

_____
_____
_____
_____
_____
_____
_____
_____
_____
_____
_____
_____
_____
_____
_____
_____
_____
_____
_____
_____

GOALS

1.

2.

3.

MONTHLY BUDGET

BILLS	GOAL	ACTUAL	CHECKING	CR

MONTH: _____

MONTHLY

RENT / MORTGAGE	$_____	$_____	☐	☐
PROPERTY INSURANCE	$_____	$_____	☐	☐
UTILITIES	$_____	$_____	☐	☐
INTERNET	$_____	$_____	☐	☐
PHONE BILL	$_____	$_____	☐	☐
HEALTH INSURANCE	$_____	$_____	☐	☐
TRANSPORTATION	$_____	$_____	☐	☐
_____	$_____	$_____	☐	☐
_____	$_____	$_____	☐	☐

SAVINGS

EMERGENCY FUND	$_____	$_____	☐	☐
RETIREMENT	$_____	$_____	☐	☐
GENERAL SAVINGS	$_____	$_____	☐	☐
_____	$_____	$_____	☐	☐
_____	$_____	$_____	☐	☐

DEBT

CREDIT CARD 1	$_____	$_____	☐	☐
CREDIT CARD 2	$_____	$_____	☐	☐
STUDENT LOANS	$_____	$_____	☐	☐
_____	$_____	$_____	☐	☐
_____	$_____	$_____	☐	☐
_____	$_____	$_____	☐	☐
_____	$_____	$_____	☐	☐
_____	$_____	$_____	☐	☐

_____
_____
_____
_____
_____
_____
_____
_____
_____
_____
_____
_____
_____
_____
_____
_____
_____
_____
_____
_____
_____
_____
_____
_____
_____
_____

MONTHLY BUDGET

BILLS	GOAL	ACTUAL	CHECKING	CRE

FOOD

	GOAL	ACTUAL	CHECKING	
GROCERIES	$_____	$_____	☐	☐
DINING OUT	$_____	$_____	☐	☐
ALCOHOL	$_____	$_____	☐	☐
COFFEE	$_____	$_____	☐	☐
_____	$_____	$_____	☐	☐
_____	$_____	$_____	☐	☐

EXTRAS

	GOAL	ACTUAL	CHECKING	
SELF CARE	$_____	$_____	☐	☐
SHOPPING	$_____	$_____	☐	☐
GIFTS	$_____	$_____	☐	☐
EVENTS	$_____	$_____	☐	☐
TRAVEL	$_____	$_____	☐	☐
CHARITABLE DONATIONS	$_____	$_____	☐	☐
_____	$_____	$_____	☐	☐
_____	$_____	$_____	☐	☐
_____	$_____	$_____	☐	☐
_____	$_____	$_____	☐	☐
_____	$_____	$_____	☐	☐

TOTAL MONEY OUT $_____

TAKE-HOME PAY $_____

SIDE HUSTLES $_____

OTHER $_____

TOTAL MONEY IN $_____

$$ IN - $$ OUT = $ _____

_____

_____

_____

_____

_____

_____

_____

_____

_____

_____

_____

_____

_____

_____

_____

_____

_____

_____

GOALS

1.

2.

3.

BILLS	GOAL	ACTUAL	CHECKING	CRE

MONTH: _____

MONTHLY

RENT / MORTGAGE	$_____	$_____	☐	☐
PROPERTY INSURANCE	$_____	$_____	☐	☐
UTILITIES	$_____	$_____	☐	☐
INTERNET	$_____	$_____	☐	☐
PHONE BILL	$_____	$_____	☐	☐
HEALTH INSURANCE	$_____	$_____	☐	☐
TRANSPORTATION	$_____	$_____	☐	☐
_____	$_____	$_____	☐	☐
_____	$_____	$_____	☐	☐

SAVINGS

EMERGENCY FUND	$_____	$_____	☐	☐
RETIREMENT	$_____	$_____	☐	☐
GENERAL SAVINGS	$_____	$_____	☐	☐
_____	$_____	$_____	☐	☐
_____	$_____	$_____	☐	☐

DEBT

CREDIT CARD 1	$_____	$_____	☐	☐
CREDIT CARD 2	$_____	$_____	☐	☐
STUDENT LOANS	$_____	$_____	☐	☐
_____	$_____	$_____	☐	☐
_____	$_____	$_____	☐	☐
_____	$_____	$_____	☐	☐
_____	$_____	$_____	☐	☐
_____	$_____	$_____	☐	☐

NOTES

MONTHLY BUDGET

BILLS	GOAL	ACTUAL	CHECKING	CRE
FOOD				
GROCERIES	$_____	$_____	☐	☐
DINING OUT	$_____	$_____	☐	☐
ALCOHOL	$_____	$_____	☐	☐
COFFEE	$_____	$_____	☐	☐
_____	$_____	$_____	☐	☐
_____	$_____	$_____	☐	☐
EXTRAS				
SELF CARE	$_____	$_____	☐	☐
SHOPPING	$_____	$_____	☐	☐
GIFTS	$_____	$_____	☐	☐
EVENTS	$_____	$_____	☐	☐
TRAVEL	$_____	$_____	☐	☐
CHARITABLE DONATIONS	$_____	$_____	☐	☐
_____	$_____	$_____	☐	☐
_____	$_____	$_____	☐	☐
_____	$_____	$_____	☐	☐
_____	$_____	$_____	☐	☐
_____	$_____	$_____	☐	☐

TOTAL MONEY OUT $_____

TAKE-HOME PAY $_____

SIDE HUSTLES $_____

OTHER $_____

TOTAL MONEY IN $_____

$$ IN - $$ OUT = $_____

_____
_____
_____
_____
_____
_____
_____
_____
_____
_____
_____
_____
_____
_____
_____
_____
_____
_____
_____

GOALS

1.

2.

3.

BILLS	GOAL	ACTUAL	CHECKING	CRE

MONTH: _____

MONTHLY

BILLS	GOAL	ACTUAL	CHECKING	CRE
RENT / MORTGAGE	$_____	$_____	☐	☐
PROPERTY INSURANCE	$_____	$_____	☐	☐
UTILITIES	$_____	$_____	☐	☐
INTERNET	$_____	$_____	☐	☐
PHONE BILL	$_____	$_____	☐	☐
HEALTH INSURANCE	$_____	$_____	☐	☐
TRANSPORTATION	$_____	$_____	☐	☐
_____	$_____	$_____	☐	☐
_____	$_____	$_____	☐	☐

SAVINGS

	GOAL	ACTUAL	CHECKING	CRE
EMERGENCY FUND	$_____	$_____	☐	☐
RETIREMENT	$_____	$_____	☐	☐
GENERAL SAVINGS	$_____	$_____	☐	☐
_____	$_____	$_____	☐	☐
_____	$_____	$_____	☐	☐

DEBT

	GOAL	ACTUAL	CHECKING	CRE
CREDIT CARD 1	$_____	$_____	☐	☐
CREDIT CARD 2	$_____	$_____	☐	☐
STUDENT LOANS	$_____	$_____	☐	☐
_____	$_____	$_____	☐	☐
_____	$_____	$_____	☐	☐
_____	$_____	$_____	☐	☐
_____	$_____	$_____	☐	☐
_____	$_____	$_____	☐	☐

MONTHLY BUDGET

BILLS	GOAL	ACTUAL	CHECKING	CR

FOOD

	GOAL	ACTUAL	CHECKING	CR
GROCERIES	$_____	$_____	☐	☐
DINING OUT	$_____	$_____	☐	☐
ALCOHOL	$_____	$_____	☐	☐
COFFEE	$_____	$_____	☐	☐
_____	$_____	$_____	☐	☐
_____	$_____	$_____	☐	☐

EXTRAS

	GOAL	ACTUAL	CHECKING	CR
SELF CARE	$_____	$_____	☐	☐
SHOPPING	$_____	$_____	☐	☐
GIFTS	$_____	$_____	☐	☐
EVENTS	$_____	$_____	☐	☐
TRAVEL	$_____	$_____	☐	☐
CHARITABLE DONATIONS	$_____	$_____	☐	☐
_____	$_____	$_____	☐	☐
_____	$_____	$_____	☐	☐
_____	$_____	$_____	☐	☐
_____	$_____	$_____	☐	☐
_____	$_____	$_____	☐	☐

TOTAL MONEY OUT $_____

TAKE-HOME PAY $_____

SIDE HUSTLES $_____

OTHER $_____

TOTAL MONEY IN $_____

$$ IN - $$ OUT = $_____

GOALS

1.

2.

3.

MONTHLY BUDGET

BILLS	GOAL	ACTUAL	CHECKING	CRE

MONTH: _____

MONTHLY

BILLS	GOAL	ACTUAL	CHECKING
RENT / MORTGAGE	$_____	$_____	☐
PROPERTY INSURANCE	$_____	$_____	☐
UTILITIES	$_____	$_____	☐
INTERNET	$_____	$_____	☐
PHONE BILL	$_____	$_____	☐
HEALTH INSURANCE	$_____	$_____	☐
TRANSPORTATION	$_____	$_____	☐
_____	$_____	$_____	☐
_____	$_____	$_____	☐

SAVINGS

	GOAL	ACTUAL	CHECKING
EMERGENCY FUND	$_____	$_____	☐
RETIREMENT	$_____	$_____	☐
GENERAL SAVINGS	$_____	$_____	☐
_____	$_____	$_____	☐
_____	$_____	$_____	☐

DEBT

	GOAL	ACTUAL	CHECKING
CREDIT CARD 1	$_____	$_____	☐
CREDIT CARD 2	$_____	$_____	☐
STUDENT LOANS	$_____	$_____	☐
_____	$_____	$_____	☐
_____	$_____	$_____	☐
_____	$_____	$_____	☐
_____	$_____	$_____	☐
_____	$_____	$_____	☐

MONTHLY BUDGET

BILLS		GOAL	ACTUAL	CHECKING	CRE
FOOD	GROCERIES	$_____	$_____	☐	☐
	DINING OUT	$_____	$_____	☐	☐
	ALCOHOL	$_____	$_____	☐	☐
	COFFEE	$_____	$_____	☐	☐
	_____	$_____	$_____	☐	☐
	_____	$_____	$_____	☐	☐
EXTRAS	SELF CARE	$_____	$_____	☐	☐
	SHOPPING	$_____	$_____	☐	☐
	GIFTS	$_____	$_____	☐	☐
	EVENTS	$_____	$_____	☐	☐
	TRAVEL	$_____	$_____	☐	☐
	CHARITABLE DONATIONS	$_____	$_____	☐	☐
	_____	$_____	$_____	☐	☐
	_____	$_____	$_____	☐	☐
	_____	$_____	$_____	☐	☐
	_____	$_____	$_____	☐	☐
	_____	$_____	$_____	☐	☐

TOTAL MONEY OUT $_____

TAKE-HOME PAY $_____

SIDE HUSTLES $_____

OTHER $_____

TOTAL MONEY IN $_____

$$ IN - $$ OUT = $ _____

_____
_____
_____
_____
_____
_____
_____
_____
_____
_____
_____
_____
_____
_____
_____
_____
_____
_____
_____
_____

GOALS

1.

2.

3.

MONTHLY BUDGET

MONTH: _____

MONTHLY

	GOAL	ACTUAL		
RENT / MORTGAGE	$_____	$_____	☐	☐
PROPERTY INSURANCE	$_____	$_____	☐	☐
UTILITIES	$_____	$_____	☐	☐
INTERNET	$_____	$_____	☐	☐
PHONE BILL	$_____	$_____	☐	☐
HEALTH INSURANCE	$_____	$_____	☐	☐
TRANSPORTATION	$_____	$_____	☐	☐
_____	$_____	$_____	☐	☐
_____	$_____	$_____	☐	☐

SAVINGS

EMERGENCY FUND	$_____	$_____	☐	☐
RETIREMENT	$_____	$_____	☐	☐
GENERAL SAVINGS	$_____	$_____	☐	☐
_____	$_____	$_____	☐	☐
_____	$_____	$_____	☐	☐

DEBT

CREDIT CARD 1	$_____	$_____	☐	☐
CREDIT CARD 2	$_____	$_____	☐	☐
STUDENT LOANS	$_____	$_____	☐	☐
_____	$_____	$_____	☐	☐
_____	$_____	$_____	☐	☐
_____	$_____	$_____	☐	☐
_____	$_____	$_____	☐	☐
_____	$_____	$_____	☐	☐

_____
_____
_____
_____
_____
_____
_____
_____
_____
_____
_____
_____
_____
_____
_____
_____
_____
_____
_____
_____
_____
_____
_____
_____

MONTHLY BUDGET

BILLS		GOAL	ACTUAL	CHECKING	CR
FOOD	GROCERIES	$_____	$_____	☐	☐
	DINING OUT	$_____	$_____	☐	☐
	ALCOHOL	$_____	$_____	☐	☐
	COFFEE	$_____	$_____	☐	☐
	_____	$_____	$_____	☐	☐
	_____	$_____	$_____	☐	☐
EXTRAS	SELF CARE	$_____	$_____	☐	☐
	SHOPPING	$_____	$_____	☐	☐
	GIFTS	$_____	$_____	☐	☐
	EVENTS	$_____	$_____	☐	☐
	TRAVEL	$_____	$_____	☐	☐
	CHARITABLE DONATIONS	$_____	$_____	☐	☐
	_____	$_____	$_____	☐	☐
	_____	$_____	$_____	☐	☐
	_____	$_____	$_____	☐	☐
	_____	$_____	$_____	☐	☐
	_____	$_____	$_____	☐	☐

TOTAL MONEY OUT $_____

TAKE-HOME PAY $_____

SIDE HUSTLES $_____

OTHER $_____

TOTAL MONEY IN $_____

$$ IN - $$ OUT = $_____

_____
_____
_____
_____
_____
_____
_____
_____
_____
_____
_____
_____
_____
_____
_____
_____
_____
_____
_____
_____

GOALS

1.

2.

3.

MONTH: _____

MONTHLY

BILLS	GOAL	ACTUAL	CHECKING
RENT / MORTGAGE	$_____	$_____	☐
PROPERTY INSURANCE	$_____	$_____	☐
UTILITIES	$_____	$_____	☐
INTERNET	$_____	$_____	☐
PHONE BILL	$_____	$_____	☐
HEALTH INSURANCE	$_____	$_____	☐
TRANSPORTATION	$_____	$_____	☐
_____	$_____	$_____	☐
_____	$_____	$_____	☐

SAVINGS

	GOAL	ACTUAL	CHECKING
EMERGENCY FUND	$_____	$_____	☐
RETIREMENT	$_____	$_____	☐
GENERAL SAVINGS	$_____	$_____	☐
_____	$_____	$_____	☐
_____	$_____	$_____	☐

DEBT

	GOAL	ACTUAL	CHECKING
CREDIT CARD 1	$_____	$_____	☐
CREDIT CARD 2	$_____	$_____	☐
STUDENT LOANS	$_____	$_____	☐
_____	$_____	$_____	☐
_____	$_____	$_____	☐
_____	$_____	$_____	☐
_____	$_____	$_____	☐
_____	$_____	$_____	☐

MONTHLY BUDGET

BILLS	GOAL	ACTUAL	CHECKING	CR

FOOD

	GOAL	ACTUAL	CHECKING	CR
GROCERIES	$_____	$_____	☐	☐
DINING OUT	$_____	$_____	☐	☐
ALCOHOL	$_____	$_____	☐	☐
COFFEE	$_____	$_____	☐	☐
_____	$_____	$_____	☐	☐
_____	$_____	$_____	☐	☐

EXTRAS

	GOAL	ACTUAL	CHECKING	CR
SELF CARE	$_____	$_____	☐	☐
SHOPPING	$_____	$_____	☐	☐
GIFTS	$_____	$_____	☐	☐
EVENTS	$_____	$_____	☐	☐
TRAVEL	$_____	$_____	☐	☐
CHARITABLE DONATIONS	$_____	$_____	☐	☐
_____	$_____	$_____	☐	☐
_____	$_____	$_____	☐	☐
_____	$_____	$_____	☐	☐
_____	$_____	$_____	☐	☐
_____	$_____	$_____	☐	☐

TOTAL MONEY OUT	$_____	
TAKE-HOME PAY	$_____	
SIDE HUSTLES	$_____	
OTHER	$_____	
TOTAL MONEY IN	$_____	

$$ IN - $$ OUT = $ _____

_____
_____
_____
_____
_____
_____
_____
_____
_____
_____
_____
_____
_____
_____
_____
_____
_____
_____
_____
_____
_____

GOALS

1.

2.

3.

BILLS	GOAL	ACTUAL	CHECKING	CRE

MONTH: _____

MONTHLY

RENT / MORTGAGE	$_____	$_____	☐	☐
PROPERTY INSURANCE	$_____	$_____	☐	☐
UTILITIES	$_____	$_____	☐	☐
INTERNET	$_____	$_____	☐	☐
PHONE BILL	$_____	$_____	☐	☐
HEALTH INSURANCE	$_____	$_____	☐	☐
TRANSPORTATION	$_____	$_____	☐	☐
_____	$_____	$_____	☐	☐
_____	$_____	$_____	☐	☐

SAVINGS

EMERGENCY FUND	$_____	$_____	☐	☐
RETIREMENT	$_____	$_____	☐	☐
GENERAL SAVINGS	$_____	$_____	☐	☐
_____	$_____	$_____	☐	☐
_____	$_____	$_____	☐	☐

DEBT

CREDIT CARD 1	$_____	$_____	☐	☐
CREDIT CARD 2	$_____	$_____	☐	☐
STUDENT LOANS	$_____	$_____	☐	☐
_____	$_____	$_____	☐	☐
_____	$_____	$_____	☐	☐
_____	$_____	$_____	☐	☐
_____	$_____	$_____	☐	☐
_____	$_____	$_____	☐	☐

MONTHLY BUDGET

BILLS	GOAL	ACTUAL	CHECKING	CRE

FOOD

	GOAL	ACTUAL	CHECKING	CRE
GROCERIES	$_____	$_____	☐	☐
DINING OUT	$_____	$_____	☐	☐
ALCOHOL	$_____	$_____	☐	☐
COFFEE	$_____	$_____	☐	☐
_____	$_____	$_____	☐	☐
_____	$_____	$_____	☐	☐

EXTRAS

	GOAL	ACTUAL	CHECKING	CRE
SELF CARE	$_____	$_____	☐	☐
SHOPPING	$_____	$_____	☐	☐
GIFTS	$_____	$_____	☐	☐
EVENTS	$_____	$_____	☐	☐
TRAVEL	$_____	$_____	☐	☐
CHARITABLE DONATIONS	$_____	$_____	☐	☐
_____	$_____	$_____	☐	☐
_____	$_____	$_____	☐	☐
_____	$_____	$_____	☐	☐
_____	$_____	$_____	☐	☐
_____	$_____	$_____	☐	☐

TOTAL MONEY OUT	$_____	
TAKE-HOME PAY	$_____	
SIDE HUSTLES	$_____	
OTHER	$_____	
TOTAL MONEY IN	$_____	

$$ IN - $$ OUT = $_____

_____
_____
_____
_____
_____
_____
_____
_____
_____
_____
_____
_____
_____
_____
_____
_____
_____
_____
_____
_____

GOALS

1.

2.

3.

MONTHLY BUDGET

BILLS	GOAL	ACTUAL	CHECKING	CR

MONTH: _____

MONTHLY

RENT / MORTGAGE	$_____	$_____	☐	☐
PROPERTY INSURANCE	$_____	$_____	☐	☐
UTILITIES	$_____	$_____	☐	☐
INTERNET	$_____	$_____	☐	☐
PHONE BILL	$_____	$_____	☐	☐
HEALTH INSURANCE	$_____	$_____	☐	☐
TRANSPORTATION	$_____	$_____	☐	☐
_____	$_____	$_____	☐	☐
_____	$_____	$_____	☐	☐

SAVINGS

EMERGENCY FUND	$_____	$_____	☐	☐
RETIREMENT	$_____	$_____	☐	☐
GENERAL SAVINGS	$_____	$_____	☐	☐
_____	$_____	$_____	☐	☐
_____	$_____	$_____	☐	☐

DEBT

CREDIT CARD 1	$_____	$_____	☐	☐
CREDIT CARD 2	$_____	$_____	☐	☐
STUDENT LOANS	$_____	$_____	☐	☐
_____	$_____	$_____	☐	☐
_____	$_____	$_____	☐	☐
_____	$_____	$_____	☐	☐
_____	$_____	$_____	☐	☐
_____	$_____	$_____	☐	☐

MONTHLY BUDGET

BILLS	GOAL	ACTUAL	CHECKING	CR

FOOD

	GOAL	ACTUAL	CHECKING	
GROCERIES	$_____	$_____	☐	☐
DINING OUT	$_____	$_____	☐	☐
ALCOHOL	$_____	$_____	☐	☐
COFFEE	$_____	$_____	☐	☐
_____	$_____	$_____	☐	☐
_____	$_____	$_____	☐	☐

EXTRAS

	GOAL	ACTUAL	CHECKING	
SELF CARE	$_____	$_____	☐	☐
SHOPPING	$_____	$_____	☐	☐
GIFTS	$_____	$_____	☐	☐
EVENTS	$_____	$_____	☐	☐
TRAVEL	$_____	$_____	☐	☐
CHARITABLE DONATIONS	$_____	$_____	☐	☐
_____	$_____	$_____	☐	☐
_____	$_____	$_____	☐	☐
_____	$_____	$_____	☐	☐
_____	$_____	$_____	☐	☐
_____	$_____	$_____	☐	☐

TOTAL MONEY OUT	$_____	
TAKE-HOME PAY	$_____	
SIDE HUSTLES	$_____	
OTHER	$_____	
TOTAL MONEY IN	$_____	

$$ IN - $$ OUT = $ _____

_____
_____
_____
_____
_____
_____
_____
_____
_____
_____
_____
_____
_____
_____
_____
_____
_____
_____
_____

GOALS

1.

2.

3.

MONTHLY BUDGET

CHAPTER TWO

WE'VE GOT DEBT, HOW 'BOUT YOU?

IF YOU'RE EVEN remotely living your life, especially if you've made a bit of a habit of not living within your means, there's a good chance you've racked up some kind of debt. If not, wait for it. It'll happen. Maybe you have student loans. Or you married someone who has student loans ("what's yours is mine" is no joke).

Maybe someone told you it was a good idea to sign up for ten different credit cards in college and now you're swimming in credit card debt. Or you want a new car, new furniture, or to buy a house someday. Debt, debt, debt. It's inevitable.

The trick is being smart about your debt. Although there's no "good" debt, there are some things that are worth going into debt for—as long as you have a solid plan for paying it off.

Bridget Casey, Founder of Money After Graduation, on "Good" Debt:

"There's no such thing as good debt. There just isn't. There's just some debt that's less bad than others. Education can be good if you're investing in a higher earning potential that you'll reap the rewards from for the rest of your working lifetime. But it's also really easy to spend on a degree you don't really like or will never use, tell yourself it's good debt, and graduate into a field where there's no jobs. In that case, it's really horrible debt."

DEBT MATTERS

Worse, debt is expensive and bad for your credit score. Let's start with why it's expensive. According to surveys by

CreditCards.com, the average credit card interest rate in 2018 was more than 16% (we're rounding here, because we're about to do some math).

If you put $1,000 on a credit card with a 16% interest rate and you don't pay the balance immediately, you'll ultimately spend more than that $1,000. For example, if you take a year to pay back that $1,000, you'll be paying more than the minimum payment each month (which is good!) but you'll also end up paying an extra $160 to the credit card company on top of the original $1,000 you spent. That's not a way to make a living, friend.

1,000 x 16% (aka 0.16) = $160

Things get worse if you only ever make the minimum payments on a card—it can take years to pay off even a small balance, and the resulting interest can end up being nearly as much as the purchase was in the first place. You can Google "credit card interest calculator" and then plug your numbers in. You'll see what I mean.

The other thing you need to know about debt is how it affects your credit score—credit and debt are inextricably connected. Your credit score is a rating assigned to your financial history to help banks, credit card companies, and other lenders assess how likely it is that you'll pay back a sum of money. Your credit worthiness is determined by a few main factors: your credit history, whether you pay your bills on time, how much you earn in a year, and two big numbers: your 1) debt-to-income ratio and 2) credit utilization ratio.

To understand your credit score you also need to understand that a ratio is a comparison of two numbers. Calculating a debt-to-income ratio is a bank's quick way of assessing your finances. The lender totals up all of your debts and compares it to your total regular income. For example, if you earn $50,000 a year, and you have a $4,000 personal loan and a $1,000 credit card balance, your total debt is $5,000. That leaves you with a debt-to-income ratio of 1:10, which calculates out to 10%.

5,000 / 50,000 = a ratio of 1:10 (aka 10%)

Your credit utilization ratio is a comparison of the total amount of credit you have available (basically all of your credit card limits added together) vs. the total amount of credit you have used (so the balance on those credit cards). If you only have one credit card with a $2,000 limit, and you've put $1,000 on that card, you have a credit utilization ratio of 50%.

1,000 / 2,000 = a ratio of 1:2 (aka 50%)

It probably does sound like we hate credit cards and we don't think anyone should ever use them (ever), and if you have debt you've messed up your whole life. But that's not quite it; credit cards can be incredibly beneficial if you use them wisely. Smart credit card use (and payment) can build your credit history, which is a crucial part of your credit score. And debt? It just happens. No matter your intentions, it will be challenging, to say the least, to really operate without getting into at least a little bit of debt.

So now that you know you can't escape your debt-ridden future, it's time to work out a plan for paying that debt off in a timely fashion. It's not enough to say, "Oh, once I start making enough money, I'll start paying off my debts." Just like how you shouldn't wait to start saving, you should never, ever, ever wait to start paying that debt off. Even the tiniest amount you can scrape together is better than nothing.

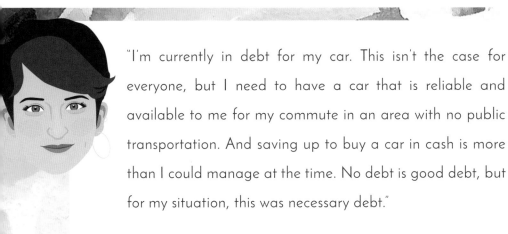

"I'm currently in debt for my car. This isn't the case for everyone, but I need to have a car that is reliable and available to me for my commute in an area with no public transportation. And saving up to buy a car in cash is more than I could manage at the time. No debt is good debt, but for my situation, this was necessary debt."

DEBT REPAYMENT STRATEGIES

What's your plan of attack? Lowest balance first? Highest interest first? Pay off one form of debt at a time? Pay them all off a little at a time? There are pros and cons to any of these methods—one of the cons being, for all of them, you have to pay down your debt with your own money, blech.

Here's a quick rundown of the rationale behind some popular approaches.

START WITH THE LOWEST BALANCE

If you pay your lowest-balance debts first, you get two main benefits:

1) The rush of having accomplished a step toward your end goal.

2) Fewer accounts to keep track of, which practically speaking, makes life easier.

That said, you'll will still be accumulating interest on your larger balances, so you may spend more on your debt in total.

START WITH THE HIGHEST INTEREST

If you work on paying down your debt with the highest interest first (which will usually be a credit card; a bank loan is typically going to have a much lower interest rate), you'll spend less money on interest over time. That makes this strategy sound like a slam dunk (and it is the strategy we use), but if your highest interest card is also your highest balance it takes discipline to stick with this strategy because you'll have to pay for so long before getting the sweet satisfaction of a $0 balance.

PAY WHATEVER, WHENEVER

If you're working on all of your debts at once (this was Meleah's old strategy), a bit at a time, you kind of get the best of neither world. Instead, you're still accruing interest on your accounts and also still having to keep up with a bunch of different bills. The reason this can work is if you need some flexibility in your debt repayment schedule.

"Having a high credit card balance stresses me OUT, so I try to pay it off as soon as I can. If I pet sit or get money for my birthday, I make a credit card payment. If I get really desperate, I dip into my savings (but I always, always, always work up a plan to rebuild)."

When it comes down to it, the best way to pay off debt is simple: it's whatever way you actually start paying down your debt. If highest interest to lowest makes sense to you, then do that. If knocking out small balances makes more sense, then go that route. Don't get hung up on the process here—just pick something that you think will work for you.

When you pick your strategy, mark it below. Then we'll work on making that strategy a reality.

MY DEBT REPAYMENT STRATEGY

✓ **LOWEST BALANCE**

✓ **HIGHEST INTEREST**

✓ **PAY WHATEVER, WHENEVER**

✓ **OTHER:** _____

HOW TO USE *DEBT REPAYMENT PLAN*

Just like the All Bills worksheet, the first step to creating your debt repayment plan is listing out your debts and jotting down a few details in a worksheet. You can write the name of the lender, the type of debt it is, or honestly just any nickname that you can remember later.

Then you'll need to look up your interest rate. You should have this info in whatever documents you recieved with your credit card or loan, but you can also look it up—usually it's in your account information.

If you can't find it, call the creditor. They definitely know exactly how much interest you've agreed to pay.

For balance, you can either write in pencil and update this section regularly, or write in pen and think of this as your balance as a "starting balance." This is honestly just up to personal preference, as long as the information is there at the end of the day.

When you have each debt accounted for, with the interest rate and balance, you're ready to look at your Goal Payoff Date. It's important to have your inventory completed before thinking about when you want to be done making payments on these suckers—because your payoff goal is dependent on your debt repayment strategy.

Cozy up to some math and start setting (realistic) goal payoff dates. For example, if you're aiming to pay off your go-to credit card first, figure out how much you can afford to throw at it, and how quickly you can whittle that balance down. Depending on how much debt you have, you may even need to set that date for a year or more in advance.

You can use the monthly boxes a few ways. You can jot down your remaining balance, your payment amounts, or, if you have small handwriting, there should also be enough room if you want to write down both.

For example, if you were to write both in the monthly box and you make a $500 payment, bringing your balance down to $1,500, you would write **500/1,500** in the allotted box.

You can also choose to plan out and write down your payments ahead of time and check off boxes as you make payments, or you can write them down as you make them and update your balance as you go.

Whatever you do in the monthly boxes, it's important that you can see your balance shrinking! It will remind you what you're working toward. That said, if for some reason you put more on a card than you pay down, log that too.

Pro Tip: You will probably want to use a pencil for the Monthly Tracker section as well. You may work out the most perfect debt repayment plan ever, but you know what they say about the best-laid plans—life gets in the way and whatnot. While it is important to sit down and create a solid plan for paying off your debts, you should expect the unexpected and stay flexible.

If something comes up and you have to revisit your monthly payment amounts, it's perfectly fine. Rome wasn't built in a day, and your student loans certainly won't be paid off in a day. Or month. Or year, probably.

DEBT	BALANCE	INTEREST RATE	GOAL PAYOFF DA
_____	$_____	_____ %	____ / __
_____	$_____	_____ %	____ / __
_____	$_____	_____ %	____ / __
_____	$_____	_____ %	____ / __
_____	$_____	_____ %	____ / __

MONTHLY TRACKER

M 1	M 2	M 3	M 4	M 5	M 6

M 7	M 8	M 9	M 10	M 11	M 12

M 1	M 2	M 3	M 4	M 5	M 6

M 7	M 8	M 9	M 10	M 11	M 12

M 1	M 2	M 3	M 4	M 5	M 6

M 7	M 8	M 9	M 10	M 11	M 12

M 1	M 2	M 3	M 4	M 5	M 6

M 7	M 8	M 9	M 10	M 11	M 12

M 1	M 2	M 3	M 4	M 5	M 6

M 7	M 8	M 9	M 10	M 11	M 12

DEBT REPAYMENT

DEBT	BALANCE	INTEREST RATE	GOAL PAYOFF DATE
_____	$_____	_____ %	____ / ____
_____	$_____	_____ %	____ / ____
_____	$_____	_____ %	____ / ____
_____	$_____	_____ %	____ / ____
_____	$_____	_____ %	____ / ____

MONTHLY TRACKER

M 1	M 2	M 3	M 4	M 5	M 6

M 7	M 8	M 9	M 10	M 11	M 12

M 1	M 2	M 3	M 4	M 5	M 6

M 7	M 8	M 9	M 10	M 11	M 12

M 1	M 2	M 3	M 4	M 5	M 6

M 7	M 8	M 9	M 10	M 11	M 12

M 1	M 2	M 3	M 4	M 5	M 6

M 7	M 8	M 9	M 10	M 11	M 12

M 1	M 2	M 3	M 4	M 5	M 6

M 7	M 8	M 9	M 10	M 11	M 12

DEBT REPAYMENT

CHAPTER THREE

EMERGENCY FUNDS 101

WE'VE TALKED A LOT about budgeting and debt repayment so far, and honestly, if you have those two things under control, you're pretty close to a solid financial setup. But "close" only counts in horseshoes and hand grenades, so we're going to need you to stick with us while we talk about building up a solid emergency fund.

An emergency fund, in a nutshell, is a stash of cash that you have set aside for—you guessed it—emergencies. This is a financial safety net that everyone needs to have.

You need an emergency fund for two main reasons:

1) If you lose your job, your emergency fund should be able to get you through three to six months.

2) Things happen. If you or a loved one gets in an accident and has medical bills, where will that money come from? If you chip a tooth and need dental work ASAP, where will that money come from? If you're not paying attention when you drive and run straight into a gutter and blow out your tire (obviously not based on personal experience at all...), where will that money come from? Your emergency fund.

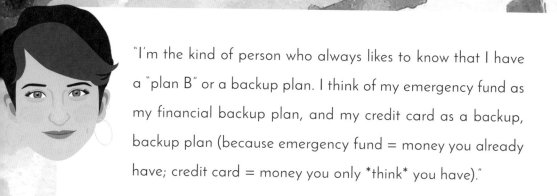

"I'm the kind of person who always likes to know that I have a "plan B" or a backup plan. I think of my emergency fund as my financial backup plan, and my credit card as a backup, backup plan (because emergency fund = money you already have; credit card = money you only *think* you have)."

But other than the obvious, what specifically qualifies as an emergency? And what doesn't?

✓ Restocking your pantry after being laid off	✗ Going out for dinner with your friends
✓ Covering unexpected medical expenses	✗ A last-minute gift for a birthday you forgot about
✓ Fixing your roof after damage from a storm	✗ A brand-new home entertainment system

THE GREAT EMERGENCY FUND VS. SAVINGS ACCOUNT DEBATE

Ideally, you should be putting about 20% of your income (at least) toward savings, but there are different types of saving you should be doing. You should have a retirement account you contribute to, a general savings account, and an emergency fund.

EMERGENCY OR NAH?

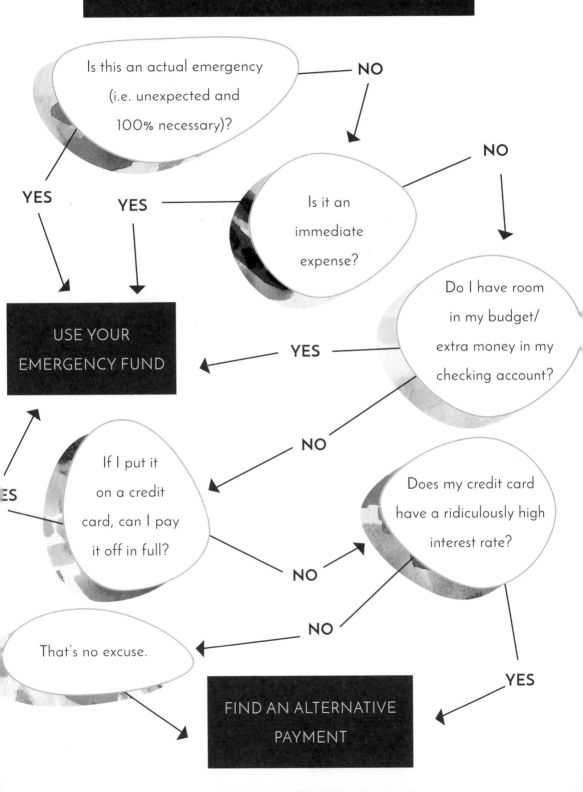

Is this an actual emergency (i.e. unexpected and 100% necessary)?

NO

YES

YES

Is it an immediate expense?

NO

NO

USE YOUR EMERGENCY FUND

YES

Do I have room in my budget/ extra money in my checking account?

ES

If I put it on a credit card, can I pay it off in full?

NO

NO

Does my credit card have a ridiculously high interest rate?

That's no excuse.

NO

YES

FIND AN ALTERNATIVE PAYMENT

An emergency fund is a place for money that you are saving, but it's different from your general savings. A savings account is actually pretty much what people normally think of when they think of a "savings account." When you're young, it's somewhere you put birthday money or occasional extra cash so you have a pile of money you can tap into when you want a new pair of shoes.

However, when you're older (aka right now, as you read this book), your savings account becomes your personal nest egg you should consistently be contributing to (which is why we included it in all thirteen of your Monthly Budget worksheets).

Whether you're saving up for a new car, a house, to go back to school, or just generally planning for your future, your savings should always be growing.

The main difference between your savings and emergency fund? You shouldn't touch your savings unless it's something specific you've saved up for; an emergency fund, however, is there specifically to cover your bases. Think of a time you had an unexpected bill crop up, and you a) borrowed money from your parents to float the cost, b) put it on a credit card and paid 20% interest, or c) didn't pay and dealt with the consequences later. These are the situations you're prepping for when you build up an emergency fund.

"In college, I was not the greatest driver, so my emergency fund ended up covering my car insurance deductible after a wreck. Twice."

That being said, in the same way that everyone has different line items in their budget, there are a couple of different options when it comes to how you do your emergency funds:

Option 1: You have separate bank accounts for your savings and emergency fund.

Option 2: You keep your savings and emergency fund in one account.

Keeping your savings and your emergency fund separated is a great way to be sure you're leaving your emergency fund alone. It's tempting to break into your emergency fund "just this once," but that is probably the worst habit you can get in to. Your emergency fund is off-limits for non-actual-emergencies, and keeping it in a separate account will make it easier to keep your grubby paws off of it. But if you have mastered the art of self-control when it comes to your finances, go forth and keep them in one account.

"I personally have my emergency fund and savings in one bank account. As long as you know how much is going in, how much is allotted for emergencies, and have a plan for building it back up, you can keep your emergency fund wherever you want!"

HOW MUCH SHOULD I SAVE?

Ultimately, how much money you have in your emergency fund is up to you, but your goal amount should be at least three months' worth of living expenses. (So if you make $40,000 annually, you'd need to put back about $10,000 into an emergency fund.) In a beautiful, wonderful, perfect world, you'd have up to six months of expenses saved up. But if you can afford to save that much, you might be better off putting it into some sort of investment account. A financial adviser can help you out.

HOW TO USE *EMERGENCY FUND*

First, use our Emergency Fund Calculator on the next page to figure out your goal amount. Then, flip to the "Going In" section of the Emergency Fund worksheet. Here, you'll plan out and track your emergency fund contributions, as well as your ongoing balance. Do you have $200 out of every paycheck automatically going to your emergency fund? *Track it!* Made a spare $100 working on a side project and you want to sock it away? *Track it.*

Every dollar you put in your emergency fund is a dollar you are investing in financial security. That's an accomplishment and this is your triumph sheet—use it.

Your emergency fund is there to help you, so don't feel bad about using it (unless it failed our Emergency or Nah Flowchart; then you should feel bad). Some months you may need to take a chunk out.

When you have to make a withdrawal from your emergency fund, you'll flip to the Going Out section and track that as well. Here, we've included a line specifically for why you took money out. The "Why Did I Spend This?" matters so you can hold yourself accountable.

You really only want to use your emergency fund for actual emergencies—not when you find a new pair of shoes you just *have* to have, or to pay for a spontaneous vacation. So hold yourself accountable here and write down exactly why you took money out of this account you worked so hard to build up. Then bust your butt to build it back up! (You'll use the "Going In" section again for that).

Also, we deliberately included more Going In spaces than Going Out. You want to be building here, not chipping away at your safety net.

EMERGENCY FUND CALCULATOR

TOTAL MONTHLY
EXPENSES (PAGE 20)

GOAL AMOUNT FOR
EMERGENCY FUND

x 3 =

GOING IN

DATE	AMOUNT	BALANCE
___ / ___	$_____	$_____
___ / ___	$_____	$_____
___ / ___	$_____	$_____
___ / ___	$_____	$_____
___ / ___	$_____	$_____
___ / ___	$_____	$_____
___ / ___	$_____	$_____
___ / ___	$_____	$_____
___ / ___	$_____	$_____
___ / ___	$_____	$_____

DATE	AMOUNT	BALANCE
___ / ___	$_____	$_____
___ / ___	$_____	$_____
___ / ___	$_____	$_____
___ / ___	$_____	$_____
___ / ___	$_____	$_____
___ / ___	$_____	$_____
___ / ___	$_____	$_____
___ / ___	$_____	$_____
___ / ___	$_____	$_____
___ / ___	$_____	$_____

EMERGENCY FUND

GOING OUT

DATE	AMOUNT	BALANCE
___ / ___	$_____	$_____
___ / ___	$_____	$_____
___ / ___	$_____	$_____
___ / ___	$_____	$_____
___ / ___	$_____	$_____
___ / ___	$_____	$_____
___ / ___	$_____	$_____
___ / ___	$_____	$_____
___ / ___	$_____	$_____
___ / ___	$_____	$_____

WHY DID I SPEND THIS?

_____

_____

_____

_____

_____

_____

_____

_____

EMERGENCY FUND

CHAPTER FOUR

BUY SMARTER

IF YOU WANT to stay on-budget (and because you've made it this far in our book you should know by now that you definitely do), you'll need to plan out your major purchases carefully—i.e. new furniture, concert tickets, a new dress and/or shoes for a wedding, gifts, etc.

Aside from how much your purchase will cost and when you'll need to buy it (which we'll get to in just a minute), you should also consider the following before making a purchase.

BEFORE YOU BUY SOMETHING, ASK YOURSELF:

1. Am I in love with it?

This is pretty much the Golden Rule of buying. If you try on a new dress and don't instantly feel like a goddess, why would you buy it? Same goes with furniture, home decor, etc. If you have to give it a good squint and convince yourself you like it, put the item back and don't walk, run.

Especially because when you do find the dress/couch/whatever that gets you feelin' yourself, you're still going to buy that, too. Then when you've spent even more money, you'll probably want to sell the old, lesser thing, which is just more work. And time = money.

2. How much does it cost?

You may need a new pair of jeans, but you don't *need* that $200 pair of jeans made from raw selvedge denim. Whether you're shopping for a new car or a new cardigan, go in with an idea of how much you want to spend. Is it high-quality? Is it actually *worth* the price tag?

"To make sure I'm spending my money well, I read reviews. I want to make sure whatever I'm buying is the best value for my money, not just the lowest price. It's worth it to me to spend 25% more if it's an item that I'll be able to keep for years to come."

3. Can I afford it?

Make sure this purchase is something you can actually afford; and not just in a put-it-on-my-credit-card-and-pay-it-off-later kind of way. If you're on a budget (which, if you haven't gotten it by now, YOU SHOULD BE ON A BUDGET), stick to your budget.

4. Will I wear/use it more than once?

If you fall in love with a crazy, neon-colored jumpsuit but you're more of a jeans kinda girl, will you really wear the jumpsuit more than once? Or at all? You may really want an espresso machine, but do you actually have time to make your own lattes in the mornings? And do you have the counter space?

On the other hand, purchases like a good, comfortable pair of shoes, or a couch, will get used a lot. Really consider the lifespan of your purchase before making it. The longer something will get used, the more (within reason) you should spend on it.

5. Do I own anything that will match it?

This goes along with "Will I wear/use it more than once?" If you buy something that doesn't match your home decor aesthetic or wardrobe, it's probably just going to sit in your closet and collect dust.

6. Do I need it or just want it?

You probably learned the difference between needing and wanting something when you were like six, but that doesn't mean you don't confuse them from time to time. We do too. But you *need* to pay your bills; you *want* to treat yo' self to a mani-pedi.

7. Is it on sale?

If not, can you wait to buy it? Pretty much everything is going to go on sale at some point, so if you can wait, you will get a better deal. If you can't wait, you should re-evaluate your budget with a hard eye to make sure you can afford it.

That said, this isn't an excuse to hit up the sale rack. If something was originally $76 and is marked down to $34, you're not saving $42; you're still spending $34. Not every deal is a good deal; you'll save a lot more money by just not buying something than you will by purchasing buy-one-get-one anything.

Mabel A. Nuñez, Founder and CEO of Girl$ on The Money, on Spending:

"If you can afford the product, you can afford the stock."

8. Can I find it somewhere else (cheaper)?

Two words: Shop. Around. Just because you fall in love with something doesn't mean there isn't a cheaper (and just-as-good version) available somewhere else. Sometimes you can find the exact same item at another store for a lower price.

9. Do I already have something similar?

Unless you're building a capsule wardrobe, you don't need ten similar black blouses. You don't need five leopard print handbags. If you already have something similar at home, don't make the purchase.

10. Am I buying it because I really like it or because I'm bored?

Just like you shouldn't go grocery shopping when you're hungry, you shouldn't go shopping when you're bored or need a little retail therapy. Plan your purchases (and your meals) out in advance to avoid any spontaneous spending.

11. How long will it last?

Nothing is made to last forever anymore, but you should still take quality into consideration when making purchases. You probably shouldn't dish out $100 for a thin sweater that will start pilling after a couple of wears, nor should you pay a pretty penny for a white microsuede couch when you have inside pets (or friends who drink red wine).

"This was a hard lesson for me to learn. I used to impulse-buy cheap clothes and accessories and justify my purchases by how inexpensive they were. But by the time summer rolled around the next year, those cheap sandals were falling apart and I had to buy a new pair.

Invest in pieces that will last a while and you'll actually end up spending less in the long-run."

HOW TO USE *PURCHASE LIST*

Now that you've asked yourself all of these questions, which purchases made the cut? Flip to the Purchase List worksheet and start planning out future purchases.

Not everything will make the cut; the time will come when you forget someone's birthday and have to pick up a last-minute gift. But for the most part, if you're going to be spending a pretty penny on something, it needs to be planned for here.

In addition to what you're purchasing, how much it costs, when you're actually purchasing it, and why, we've included a "Priority" column. Setting priorities is important because it reframes things in terms of choices instead of deprivation.

You're not going without something you want—you're just delaying it until you've taken care of everything else.

You'll color in the circles according to importance—one circle if it's not an important purchase (i.e. something you want but don't need, like a bigger TV), or five circles if it's something you need to buy ASAP (like a gift for an upcoming birthday or event or new furniture after a move).

Setting these priorities will help you figure out which purchases to plan and save for first.

If you really want to get artsy with it (and if you already enjoy planning things out on paper the old-fashioned way, there's a good chance you do), you could color code your circle system. Five circles gets your favorite pen, and so on.

PURCHASE	HOW MUCH	DATE	PRIORITY
_____	$ _____	__ / __	○ ○ ○ ○
_____	$ _____	__ / __	○ ○ ○ ○
_____	$ _____	__ / __	○ ○ ○ ○
_____	$ _____	__ / __	○ ○ ○ ○
_____	$ _____	__ / __	○ ○ ○ ○
_____	$ _____	__ / __	○ ○ ○ ○
_____	$ _____	__ / __	○ ○ ○ ○
_____	$ _____	__ / __	○ ○ ○ ○
_____	$ _____	__ / __	○ ○ ○ ○
_____	$ _____	__ / __	○ ○ ○ ○
_____	$ _____	__ / __	○ ○ ○ ○
_____	$ _____	__ / __	○ ○ ○ ○
_____	$ _____	__ / __	○ ○ ○ ○
_____	$ _____	__ / __	○ ○ ○ ○
_____	$ _____	__ / __	○ ○ ○ ○

PURCHASE LIST

PURCHASE	HOW MUCH	DATE	PRIORITY
_____	$ _____	__ / __	○ ○ ○ ○
_____	$ _____	__ / __	○ ○ ○ ○
_____	$ _____	__ / __	○ ○ ○ ○
_____	$ _____	__ / __	○ ○ ○ ○
_____	$ _____	__ / __	○ ○ ○ ○
_____	$ _____	__ / __	○ ○ ○ ○
_____	$ _____	__ / __	○ ○ ○ ○
_____	$ _____	__ / __	○ ○ ○ ○
_____	$ _____	__ / __	○ ○ ○ ○
_____	$ _____	__ / __	○ ○ ○ ○
_____	$ _____	__ / __	○ ○ ○ ○
_____	$ _____	__ / __	○ ○ ○ ○
_____	$ _____	__ / __	○ ○ ○ ○
_____	$ _____	__ / __	○ ○ ○ ○
_____	$ _____	__ / __	○ ○ ○ ○

PURCHASE LIST

CHAPTER FIVE

SETTING FINANCIAL GOALS

NOW THAT YOU'RE FAMILIAR with budgeting, saving, and making overall smart financial decisions, and you have an idea of where you are financially, it's time to set some goals for yourself. Although this workbook is completely undated, the idea is that it will get you through an entire year; so think about what you want to get better at financially this year. What could you realistically achieve?

First, you're going to create what we like to call a "brain dump." Whatever financial goals come to mind first, scribble them down.

This could include literally anything, short-term and/or long-term—like "getting out of debt," "paying off the new TV," "making it through a month-long no-spending challenge," or even "start investing this year." Whatever financial improvements you want to make, no matter how big or small, write 'em down.

"When I graduated college, I moved back home with the intention of building up my savings, so I set a goal amount and a timeline—I only lived there for a year and a half, and I saved half of every paycheck. If you can move back in with your parents, I highly recommend it; but if that's not feasible, get a bunch of roommates, move to an inexpensive apartment, and cut some major expenses—just do what's realistic for you."

You may have noticed that we haven't touched on investing; we're taking financial baby steps here, but if you're ready to dip your toe in and set some goals around investing, here's a quick rundown:

Mabel A. Nuñez, Founder and CEO of Girl$ on The Money, on Investing For Beginners:

"My quick investing tip for beginners would be to make sure you are prepared to invest. It's not just something anyone should jump into.

1. Get rid of lingering credit card debt/consumer debt.

2. Live frugally so you can save.

3. Have your emergency fund separate from your investing fund.

4. As a first investment, I would recommend either a diversified S&P 500 index fund with a low-expense ratio or a few shares of your favorite company—as long as you feel the company will be around for a long time.

5. Stay away from junk—and that includes penny stocks or the 'latest fad.'"

HOW TO USE FINANCIAL GOALS

After you've finished the "Brain Dump" section, get ready to prioritize your financial goals in your Financial Goals worksheet. Consider which goals would be the easiest and quickest to achieve, as well as which goals would improve your financial state the most. Then choose your top four financial goals.

Keep your financial goals realistic. You probably can't pay off all of your student loans in one year, and you might not be able to live too beneath your means if your apartment is $3,000 a month. It's the little things that add up over time, so it's okay to start small if you think you need to. (But also... find a cheaper apartment. Or a roommate. Or a few.)

Once you've chosen your top four, set a few short-term goals for achieving them. A goal without a plan is just a wish, or at least that's what all the inspirational posters say.

Also consider how long each goal will take you. One month? Six months? A year? Remember that you can go back through your monthly budget sheets and incorporate these short-term goals so you have more concrete steps for achieving them.

If you're not sure how to achieve your goals, revisit some of the worksheets you've already done. Is there room in your budget that you could direct toward this goal? Is your nine-to-five salary tapped out, but you have a skill you could channel into a side hustle so you have some extra money to work with?

Where there's a will, there's a way (as long as you have a little patience).

"When I set the goal to pay down my highest-interest credit card, I decided to start dogsitting and babysitting again so I'd have more income. Then I made sure not to let my extra money go to coffee runs (WHICH WAS TEMPTING) but, instead, toward paying down my credit card balance."

BRAIN DUMP

BRAIN DUMP

FINANCIAL GOALS

1.

TIME FRAME: _____

STEPS TO TAKE:

- _____

- _____

- _____

2.

TIME FRAME: _____

STEPS TO TAKE:

- _____

- _____

- _____

3.

TIME FRAME: _____

STEPS TO TAKE:

- _____
- _____
- _____

4.

TIME FRAME: _____

STEPS TO TAKE:

- _____
- _____
- _____

FINANCIAL GOALS

CHAPTER SIX

PUTTING IT ALL TOGETHER

YOU'VE MADE IT! No matter how you got here—whether you skipped around the worksheets or you read everything word for word (we highly recommend the latter, of course)—you've made some *major* financial progress.

Now it's time to see just *how much* progress you've made over the past year. Because we're not your moms or your financial advisers, we're not going to stalk your bank accounts and give you a gold star. Instead, you'll have to do this yourself.

Over the course of this book, you've read about:

• Creating a budget

• Debt repayment strategies

• Building a savings and emergency fund

• Setting smart, realistic goals

And now you're ready to connect all of the dots.

We're big believers in assessment (in case you didn't know that by now). You filled out the Financial Self-Assessment worksheet at the beginning of this book; on the following page, you'll record the state of your finances as they are now, a year later. Then you're going to do a little math.

In the bubbles, you'll record the increase or decrease in your savings, emergency fund, credit score, and debt, and you'll check in with your goal progress. Feel free to doodle here as well—you can give yourself a gold star!

1. Did you keep a monthly budget?

| YES | NO |

2. Do you have a savings strategy?

| YES | NO |

If yes, how much money is in your savings account?

_____

3. Do you have a separate emergency fund?

| YES | NO |

If yes, how much money is in your emergency fund?

_____

4. What's your credit score now?

_____

5. Do you have debt?

| YES | NO |

If yes, how much do you owe?

_____

FINAL SELF-ASSESSMENT

My savings account has increased by:

My debt has decreased by:

My credit score has increased by:

My emergency fund has increased by:

Goal 1 progress:

Goal 2 progress:

Goal 4 progress:

Goal 3 progress:

But because we don't know how to let things go, we're going to leave you with a few more final pieces of financial wisdom:

1. Paying your bills gets A LOT easier when you set up auto-pay.

Obviously, you should still check each month to make sure your payments are going through. But with auto-pay, there's a much higher chance you won't miss any payments.

"I set up auto-transfers for my savings years ago and it's the best thing I've ever done financially—and the easiest. I don't even think about moving money to my savings; I just log in every so often and marvel at how much the amount has grown."

2. This also applies to your savings and emergency fund.

Set up auto-transfers so moving that money over won't even be a question; this way, there's no opportunity to not move it over because you thought you had more money than you did and then went on an impromptu shopping spree instead.

3. Try to only put what you can pay off at the end of each month on your credit card.

Credit card debt is hands-down the easiest form of debt to rack up if you're not constantly tracking it.

4. Don't wait to start saving for your future. Don't wait to start paying off your debt.

Your future starts now. You should be doing everything included in this workbook at the same time; it can be overwhelming at first, but you'll thank us later.

5. Talk to your friends about your finances.

Or your family. Or your significant other. Just make sure someone knows your financial state, what your goals are, and will hold you accountable. You're more likely to show up to a workout class if your friend is going too, right? Literally everything is easier with a friend.

"Honestly, talking to Elise about my credit card balances was the first time I'd buckled down and faced them. So when we tell you friend-accountability is important, it is because we're living it."

And with that, we leave the rest to you.

All of these workbook pages are undated, so if you miss logging a payment or abandon the whole thing for three months, you can always pick up right where you left off without wasting pages.

As we've said a million times throughout this book, this is your financial journey—it's going to be a long, bumpy road, and you'll inevitably veer off course and have to find your way back a couple of times. But unlike with your ex, you should always come back to your budget.

NOTES, EXTRAS, & MORE

MESSED UP A PAGE? Need more space for your financial planning? We've included some extra worksheets back here for you to use, as well as notes pages—because everybody needs a place for random thoughts, tidbits of information, and two password spots for when you finally update it for the first time since 2006.

BILLS	AMOUNT	DUE	CHECKING	CRE

MONTHLY

BILLS	AMOUNT	DUE	CHECKING	CRE
RENT/MORTGAGE	$_____	_____	☐	☐
PROPERTY INSURANCE	$_____	_____	☐	☐
UTILITIES	$_____	_____	☐	☐
INTERNET	$_____	_____	☐	☐
PHONE BILL	$_____	_____	☐	☐
HEALTH INSURANCE	$_____	_____	☐	☐
TRANSPORTATION	$_____	_____	☐	☐
_____	$_____	_____	☐	☐
_____	$_____	_____	☐	☐

DEBT

BILLS	AMOUNT	DUE	CHECKING	CRE
CREDIT CARD 1	$_____	_____	☐	☐
CREDIT CARD 2	$_____	_____	☐	☐
STUDENT LOANS	$_____	_____	☐	☐
_____	$_____	_____	☐	☐
_____	$_____	_____	☐	☐
_____	$_____	_____	☐	☐

MISC.

BILLS	AMOUNT	DUE	CHECKING	CRE
MEMBERSHIPS	$_____	_____	☐	☐
TAXES	$_____	_____	☐	☐
_____	$_____	_____	☐	☐
_____	$_____	_____	☐	☐
_____	$_____	_____	☐	☐
_____	$_____	_____	☐	☐
_____	$_____	_____	☐	☐

TOTAL BILLS $_____

ALL BILLS

MONTH: _____

MONTHLY

	GOAL	ACTUAL	CHECKING	
RENT / MORTGAGE	$_____	$_____	☐	☐
PROPERTY INSURANCE	$_____	$_____	☐	☐
UTILITIES	$_____	$_____	☐	☐
INTERNET	$_____	$_____	☐	☐
PHONE BILL	$_____	$_____	☐	☐
HEALTH INSURANCE	$_____	$_____	☐	☐
TRANSPORTATION	$_____	$_____	☐	☐
_____	$_____	$_____	☐	☐
_____	$_____	$_____	☐	☐

SAVINGS

	GOAL	ACTUAL	CHECKING	
EMERGENCY FUND	$_____	$_____	☐	☐
RETIREMENT	$_____	$_____	☐	☐
GENERAL SAVINGS	$_____	$_____	☐	☐
_____	$_____	$_____	☐	☐
_____	$_____	$_____	☐	☐

DEBT

	GOAL	ACTUAL	CHECKING	
CREDIT CARD 1	$_____	$_____	☐	☐
CREDIT CARD 2	$_____	$_____	☐	☐
STUDENT LOANS	$_____	$_____	☐	☐
_____	$_____	$_____	☐	☐
_____	$_____	$_____	☐	☐
_____	$_____	$_____	☐	☐
_____	$_____	$_____	☐	☐
_____	$_____	$_____	☐	☐

MONTHLY BUDGET

BILLS	GOAL	ACTUAL	CHECKING	CRE
FOOD				
GROCERIES	$_____	$_____	☐	☐
DINING OUT	$_____	$_____	☐	☐
ALCOHOL	$_____	$_____	☐	☐
COFFEE	$_____	$_____	☐	☐
_____	$_____	$_____	☐	☐
_____	$_____	$_____	☐	☐
EXTRAS				
SELF CARE	$_____	$_____	☐	☐
SHOPPING	$_____	$_____	☐	☐
GIFTS	$_____	$_____	☐	☐
EVENTS	$_____	$_____	☐	☐
TRAVEL	$_____	$_____	☐	☐
CHARITABLE DONATIONS	$_____	$_____	☐	☐
_____	$_____	$_____	☐	☐
_____	$_____	$_____	☐	☐
_____	$_____	$_____	☐	☐
_____	$_____	$_____	☐	☐
_____	$_____	$_____	☐	☐

TOTAL MONEY OUT $_____

TAKE-HOME PAY $_____

SIDE HUSTLES $_____

OTHER $_____

TOTAL MONEY IN $_____

WHAT'S LEFT? $ _____

NOTES

MONTHLY BUDGET

GOALS

1.

2.

3.

DEBT	BALANCE	INTEREST RATE	GOAL PAYOFF DA
_____	$_____	_____ %	____ / ___
_____	$_____	_____ %	____ / ___
_____	$_____	_____ %	____ / ___
_____	$_____	_____ %	____ / ___
_____	$_____	_____ %	____ / ___

MONTHLY TRACKER

M 1	M 2	M 3	M 4	M 5	M 6

M 7	M 8	M 9	M 10	M 11	M 12

M 1	M 2	M 3	M 4	M 5	M 6

M 7	M 8	M 9	M 10	M 11	M 12

M 1	M 2	M 3	M 4	M 5	M 6

M 7	M 8	M 9	M 10	M 11	M 12

M 1	M 2	M 3	M 4	M 5	M 6

M 7	M 8	M 9	M 10	M 11	M 12

M 1	M 2	M 3	M 4	M 5	M 6

M 7	M 8	M 9	M 10	M 11	M 12

DEBT REPAYMENT

GOING IN

DATE	AMOUNT	BALANCE
___ / ___	$_____	$_____
___ / ___	$_____	$_____
___ / ___	$_____	$_____
___ / ___	$_____	$_____
___ / ___	$_____	$_____
___ / ___	$_____	$_____
___ / ___	$_____	$_____
___ / ___	$_____	$_____
___ / ___	$_____	$_____
___ / ___	$_____	$_____

DATE	AMOUNT	BALANCE
___ / ___	$_____	$_____
___ / ___	$_____	$_____
___ / ___	$_____	$_____
___ / ___	$_____	$_____
___ / ___	$_____	$_____
___ / ___	$_____	$_____
___ / ___	$_____	$_____
___ / ___	$_____	$_____
___ / ___	$_____	$_____
___ / ___	$_____	$_____

EMERGENCY FUND

GOING OUT

DATE	AMOUNT	BALANCE
___ / ___	$_____	$_____
___ / ___	$_____	$_____
___ / ___	$_____	$_____
___ / ___	$_____	$_____
___ / ___	$_____	$_____
___ / ___	$_____	$_____
___ / ___	$_____	$_____
___ / ___	$_____	$_____
___ / ___	$_____	$_____
___ / ___	$_____	$_____

WHY DID I SPEND THIS?

_____

_____

_____

_____

_____

_____

_____

_____

EMERGENCY FUND

PURCHASE	HOW MUCH	DATE	PRIORITY
_____	$ _____	__ / __	○ ○ ○ ○
_____	$ _____	__ / __	○ ○ ○ ○
_____	$ _____	__ / __	○ ○ ○ ○
_____	$ _____	__ / __	○ ○ ○ ○
_____	$ _____	__ / __	○ ○ ○ ○
_____	$ _____	__ / __	○ ○ ○ ○
_____	$ _____	__ / __	○ ○ ○ ○
_____	$ _____	__ / __	○ ○ ○ ○
_____	$ _____	__ / __	○ ○ ○ ○
_____	$ _____	__ / __	○ ○ ○ ○
_____	$ _____	__ / __	○ ○ ○ ○
_____	$ _____	__ / __	○ ○ ○ ○
_____	$ _____	__ / __	○ ○ ○ ○
_____	$ _____	__ / __	○ ○ ○ ○
_____	$ _____	__ / __	○ ○ ○ ○

PURCHASE LIST

BRAIN DUMP

FINANCIAL GOALS

1.

TIME FRAME: _____

STEPS TO TAKE:

- _____
- _____
- _____

2.

TIME FRAME: _____

STEPS TO TAKE:

- _____
- _____
- _____

TIME FRAME: _____

STEPS TO TAKE:

- _____
- _____
- _____

TIME FRAME: _____

STEPS TO TAKE:

- _____
- _____
- _____

FINANCIAL GOALS

NOTES

NOTES

NOTES

NOTES

NOTES

NOTES

NOTES

NOTES

NOTES

NOTES

NOTES

NOTES

NOTES

NOTES

NOTES

NOTES

NOTES

ABOUT THE AUTHORS

ELISE WILLIAMS | @melisewilliams
Elise is the Co-Founder and Editor of Earn Spend
Live—although when binge-watching *Sailor Moon* and
eating frozen pizza becomes a profitable career, she'll
leave the world of digital publishing behind. She holds
a BA in technical writing from The University of
Central Arkansas and resides in Maumelle, AR,
with her cat Lazarus.

MELEAH BOWLES | @meleahbowle
Meleah is the other Co-Founder of Earn Spend Live. Using
her feminine wiles and maybe a touch of black magic, sh
tricked her partner into moving one block away from he
mother in Conway, AR, with their two dogs and a ferret.
because why not? She and Elise have known each other fo
years, but only recently discovered their undying
love for each other. She, too, has a BA in technica
writing from The University of Central Arkansas